I Took a Chance

GARY R. GRAY

WESTBOW
PRESS®
A DIVISION OF THOMAS NELSON
& ZONDERVAN

WestBow Press books may be ordered through booksellers or by contacting:

WestBow Press
A Division of Thomas Nelson & Zondervan
1663 Liberty Drive
Bloomington, IN 47403
www.westbowpress.com
844-714-3454

Because of the dynamic nature of the Internet, any web addresses or links contained in this book may have changed since publication and may no longer be valid. The views expressed in this work are solely those of the author and do not necessarily reflect the views of the publisher, and the publisher hereby disclaims any responsibility for them.

Any people depicted in stock imagery provided by Getty Images are models, and such images are being used for illustrative purposes only. Certain stock imagery © Getty Images.

ISBN: 978-1-6642-9137-9 (sc)
ISBN: 978-1-6642-9138-6 (e)

Library of Congress Control Number: 2023902016

Print information available on the last page.

WestBow Press rev. date: 02/28/2023

Acknowledgments

FIRST OF ALL, I MUST thank my sister, Dede Connor, for gifting Chance to me. It was good for Chance, good for Dede, and good for me. I continue to update her on his status, progress, and antics. Dede has been around horses all her life and is well respected as a knowledgeable equestrian.

I must also thank my friend and fellow Praise Team member Erin Wurst for her assistance in editing the initial manuscript. In addition to being an accomplished horse owner, she is an English and History teacher. She was able to provide valuable suggestions as we worked through the manuscript.

I must especially thank my wife, Patty Gray for her assistance. Patty is an animal lover and adores her cats and chickens. She also helps to take care of Chance, feeding him and walking him over to the south pasture. Patty is also a very good proofreader and has assisted in getting the manuscript ready for submission.

Introduction

MY OBSERVATION IS THAT AS each person is unique, so each animal has their unique traits. While each horse may look similar to another horse, each horse has its own personality.

In the days of my youth, our family time focused around our horses. We rode them most of the weekend, competed in various horse shows, and enjoyed trail rides. In the fall, we hunted from horseback.

Early on, we learned to respect our horses, care for them, and to understand that each horse is different. The discipline and responsibility of caring for these horses was especially helpful in our growth and development.

As I began to prepare for college and my chosen career path, it seemed unlikely that I would be able to continue with horses. My sister Dede, now Dede Connor, took over much of the responsibility for our horses and continued caring for them. Today she has a nice place with several horses on the property.

Finding myself approaching "retirement," my wife and I had moved to a rural setting and had some space. When Dede suggested taking on one of the horses, it seemed like an interesting idea. I found that the horse was even more interesting.

The horse, Chance, is a registered Paint Horse. They have either black or brown patches on a basically white coat, as if spattered with paint. He is actually a very nice looking horse. He and I seemed to get along well from the start.

Chance is bright-eyed and alert. He seems especially interested in people and, as far as I know, has never met a stranger. On our rides he wants to meet the people we come across. Part of this may be that some give him cookies, but he is just glad to have attention. In fact, he often demands attention, but does so in endearing ways. He will come to the gate put his head over and whicker or come across the pasture to nuzzle you as you add water to the trough. Just a big, friendly sort who likes to be in your hip pocket.

I have enjoyed a relationship with a number of horses, but my relationship with Chance has been different — special. That is why I decided to write this book. I believe that people who know horses will find it interesting and it may remind them of a special horse in their life. For those who have not yet known the joy of such a relationship, perhaps they will be inspired and encouraged to reach out to such a noble animal and discover the various facets of their personality.

Chance is a friend, a companion, a tease, and an entertainer for me. He has a bit of a mischievous streak, as Dede calls it, "Dennis the Menace." Just when you think you know all of his tricks, he comes up with a new one. All in all, it is great just to spend time with him.

Contents

A Horse Comes Home

LOOKING FOR A SIMPLER LIFE and preparing for retirement, Patty and I moved to a quiet, rural area in North Florida where we acquired a nice house on an acre and a half of land and soon developed a large vegetable garden out back. I had access to a large hunting lease across the road and enjoyed riding through the woods on the side-by-side and making food plots for the deer with the tractor.

Patty was concerned that the lot next to us would someday have a house with neighbors closer than we liked, so after much consideration we bought the lot. By this time, I had acquired several tractor implements and a trailer to haul the tractor, and I decided to fence the lot with a vision of having a building to keep the trailer and other items out of the weather.

It was sometime during the fencing of this lot that we began to think it would be nice to have a horse on the lot. Patty's brother thought we were making a mistake and told us of folks he knew who "had money" and often complained about how much it cost to keep a horse. One of our neighbors said we would be better off getting a couple of cows to put in the pasture. I admit that I was a little concerned about the costs as I prepared to retire: the cost of the fence, the cost of the barn, the cost of building materials, the cost of the feed and farriers, and the vet bills.

Horse people know it's not about the cost, though; it's about the relationship. There is a bond of trust and respect like no other between a man and his horse. The horse and the rider depend on each other.

Those moments of quiet contemplation in connection with your trusted ride are worth everything. And competing at events as partners is so special. Victory is that much sweeter when shared with such a partner. Losses are put in perspective by your trusted friend and companion. To have such a friend come to the gate to greet you when you come home is a special feeling.

I don't know if my sister Dede Connor knew about this, but she and her husband began to talk to us about taking Chance, a registered Paint Horse that she had ridden for a few years.

Dede had a couple of other horses, and Chance just wasn't getting much exercise. She explained he was getting over some soreness in his stifle joint, and the vet believed he would make a full recovery. Chance was about twelve years old.

I remember thinking that at my age—sixty-four—Chance and I could probably ride together about as long as we were both able. I also was a bit skeptical of the deal, which included my old roping saddle that I had ridden as a teenager as well as several other pieces of tack. When I asked Dede about it, she said she wanted to reduce her feed bill and have Chance get some exercise. "Don't look a gift horse in the mouth" is the old adage.

At Thanksgiving, we went to have dinner with Dede and her husband, Gary. We stayed over to have an opportunity to take Chance for a ride. As I mentioned, he is a Paint horse, about fifteen hands tall with very nice conformation. Paints have large patches of dark brown or black on a white coat, and at fifteen hands, a hand being four inches, he stands five feet tall at the shoulder. He is generally very well-mannered, steady, and easygoing. Chance does have a bit of extrovert in him; however, he may be a little too smart for his own good. Dede calls him "Dennis the Menace." But more on that later.

The day after Thanksgiving was a nice mild Florida day, and the ride went well along the sandy roads surrounding Dede's place. I noticed that she bridled him with a hackamore, and I saddled him with my old roping saddle. I felt an immediate bond with this horse as he reminded me of one of the special horses of my youth. There was a moment when I reached down and gave him a pat on the neck and called him "Champ" by mistake. I must admit that my eyes moistened a bit as I realized the connection.

Champ had been the registered Quarter Horse of my youth. He was a strawberry roan, smart, gentle, and wanting to please. He was about four years old, and I was fifteen when we started out together. We rode everywhere together. One summer we spent so much time together working on leg and voice commands that I was able to take him into a ring, slip the hackamore off, and have him respond, even to a sliding stop with just leg and voice commands.

On Friday nights, we would all go up to the rodeo arena and practice different games. One year, one of the old hands organized a quadrille on horseback for us to perform at our local rodeo. My partner and I were the leaders. The most exciting feature was the flying figure eight. In this maneuver the riders from one corner were instructed to keep a steady pace and a good gap so the riders from the other corner could adjust accordingly. It was a great foolproof plan – when it worked.

One practice I was approaching the crossing point from the "keep it steady" side. The other rider was lagging behind, and I knew we would collide if I stayed at this pace. At fifteen, I was proud of my horse and what he could do, and I just knew we could fix this. But just as I let him out to go ahead, the other rider urged their horse forward. I don't think I had ever seen a horse move so fast! I immediately reined Champ into a sliding stop, and the horses and riders came together with one running flat out and one trying to stop.

Champ spun around and was knocked on his side and started to roll. I remember watching the saddle horn as it came toward my chest, then he rolled back. I immediately jumped up and pulled my leg out from under him. Fearing the worst, I asked him up to his feet, and we walked around for a few moments.

Seeing that Champ was okay, I vaulted up into the saddle. People kept coming by to ask if I was okay and I kept trying to pass it off as most young cowboys would. Miraculously, both horses and riders seemed to be all right except for a few bruises. I had noticed my left leg would start to shake, but it finally quit. We performed the maneuver the next day for the rodeo without incident. (As I look back, I blame this incident for the arthritis that formed in my left hip, which required some surgery years later.)

Then the day came for me to go off to college. I entrusted Champ to Dede's care. As a teenager she was already a very accomplished horsewoman. I didn't have much hope of returning to riding as the career path I had chosen would probably just barely support me, let alone a horse and a place to keep him.

Back in the '70s, Florida struggled with the problem of swamp fever, otherwise known as equine infectious anemia. We had lots of biting flies and mosquitoes, so even with diligent effort to keep repellant on the horses it was hard to keep some of them from getting the disease. There was no vaccine or cure in those days. At one time I had considered becoming a veterinarian so that I could search for one. We lost several horses to this illness.

And so it was with Champ. While I was away at college, he came down with the disease.

I think Dede felt that she may have let me and Champ down, but it wasn't her fault; it was just part of dealing with horses in Florida at the time. As I pondered accepting Dede's offer of Chance, I wondered if she might be trying to make things up to me.

Chance and I felt a real bond right from the start. He's really like a big dog in some ways, following people around, taking stock of what they are doing. It seemed like it would be nice to have the big guy around.

I brought the old saddle home with me and immediately started working it over with saddle soap and oil. I even went online and bought a new cinch strap and billet strap for the girth. For those of you who aren't familiar, these are the items that are *supposed* to keep the saddle in place. More about this on our first ride.

We pressed ahead with a building on the new lot that would accommodate a couple of stalls, a place for the trailer, tractor implements, and a tack room. All of this during hunting season and looking after the fall garden.

The first thing we did was to build out the stalls, one twelve-by-fifteen-foot stall for Chance and another twelve-by-ten-foot stall with a walkway in between to separate the stalls and give us a place to feed from. No sooner had we finished this when I realized I would need a way to keep the curious, extroverted Chance out of the tractor implements and away from the trailer. I decided to use some heavy rope with light line to keep it together. For the most part Chance respected this.

I designed the tack room and started building. Fortunately, or perhaps, providentially, schedules did not line up for Dede to bring Chance over until January. Just before he was to come, I was still working on the tack room and Dede called to say that he had scraped his foreleg and she needed some time to doctor it. We put things off until February and I took a couple of days off to complete the tack room and put a fence around the tractor implements.

Chance arrived February 10th. He walked out of the trailer, looked around, and calmly started to graze on what grass was available. His stall was ready, covered in pine shavings with a plug of coastal and a plug of alfalfa hay waiting for him. While Dede and Patty talked, I rode out through the hunting lease on the side-by-side with Dede's husband Gary. When we returned, I barely had time to take notes on the feed mix and leg treatment before Dede and Gary were ready to leave.

I don't think I mentioned it, but Gary Connor is really into tractors. The guy is an amazing mechanic and can seemingly take a pile of rusty bolts and metal and restore them to a working machine. They were planning to drive down to south Florida to pick up an old tractor the next day and he was anxious to get home and get things ready for the trip.

Chance didn't seem to mind being left and spent the afternoon looking around and eating... and eating... and eating. I decided to let him settle in for the day rather than going for a ride. When it came time for him to have his evening feed, he had a little trouble figuring out how to get into the stall. Dede's stalls face the breeze way, mine go along side. Being driven by his desire for his grain, he eventually figured it out and was standing at the ready.

Dede had said she fed him at 6:30 a.m. and 6:30 p.m. This wasn't going to work out right away as I leave for work at about 5:30 a.m. However, the next day was a Sunday, and I went over to the barn to feed him at his usual time, he immediately came in from the field to his stall.

As I said, he is smart and much like a big friendly dog. It didn't take him long to be waiting for me at the gate each morning. As I walked to the barn he would walk right beside me, as if on a lead. Arriving at the barn, I would motion him around to the stall as I went in to get his feed ready.

I found myself looking forward to these encounters and enjoying the company. Often when I would pull in the driveway, Chance would come to the gate and whicker a greeting. It was just impossible to go into the house without going over and patting his neck.

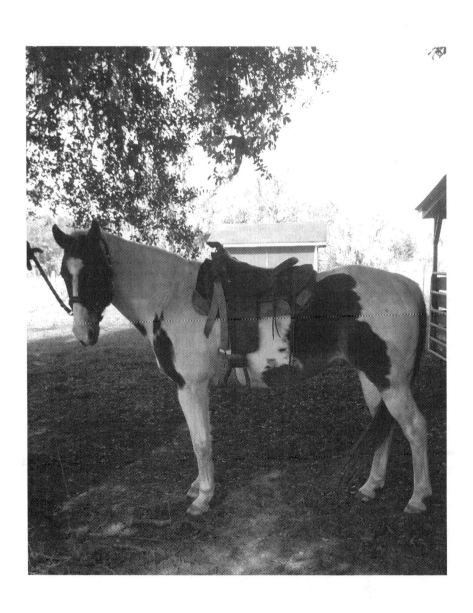

The First Ride

BIG BROTHERS WOULD DO WELL to listen to the advice of their little sisters. As I said, I am in my 60's with my sister the horse woman close behind. She recommended this thing called a "mounting block" which we had used at her place for our ride. I thought about it and decided an old cowboy like me didn't need to worry with such things.

After church, I hurried home to saddle up Chance for our first ride. Patty usually goes to the grocery store after church, so I was going to be on my own with Chance. There is a state road that I had to cross to get to the hunting lease where I planned to ride, and it is frequented by large trucks. Dede had said Chance isn't too much bothered by such things, but to be on the safe side, my plan was to lead him across the road and down to the lease.

To be sure we were still on good terms, I was going to ride him a bit in the pasture before going out the gate and down the road. This meant that I would have to mount and dismount a couple of times. No problem for an old cowboy and quadrille leader like me, right?

It's amazing how much you can forget over the course of 45 years. Things you do almost by instinct seem to fade right out of your mind. You know, little things like how a horse will swell his belly when you are tightening the girth, or just exactly where the saddle should be placed.

Dede takes great care of all her animals. Chance came to me with a few extra pounds that he probably didn't need. At least, the old saddle didn't need those pounds. The horse almost seemed to have no withers.

Chance stood patiently while I put the saddle on him and dropped his head into the bridle with no problem. The saddle was rigged in the "full" position with options for seven-eighths and three-quarter. This option allows the saddle to be placed a little forward of the standard rig if needed. On each side of the saddle were two attachment points for the billet strap and cinch strap. This afforded the option of where to place the saddle and still have the girth in the proper place under the horse. I couldn't remember how I had used it before with Champ, so I opted to leave it in the full position.

Everything seemed good and, without walking him around or double checking the cinch strap, I stepped up into the saddle – which immediately slipped. I couldn't get my foot into the offhand stirrup quick enough to right things. Chance went right and I went left. I didn't land all that hard and still had the reins in my hands. It was a sobering reminder that I wasn't as up on riding as I had been 45 years ago, but no harm done. I felt fine and Chance seemed okay.

Chance and I still seemed to be friends, so I led him back over to the hitching post, loosened the girth, and righted the saddle. As you might have guessed, the girth had been a bit loose, so I snugged it up a notch. I also pulled out the manure bucket to stand on while I made another attempt to mount. This one was successful, and we rode around the pasture a bit. All seemed to be well, so we headed for the gate.

As I said, Chance is generally well-mannered. He was patient with my dismount and moved around easily as we moved through the gate. Following my plan, I walked him across and down the road to the lease. Again, Chance moved though this gate easily and without incident.

I was beginning to be a believer in the "mounting block" idea. Maybe this is a good thing for older, uh… heavier cowboys. I led Chance around to a little mound of dirt and mounted. We were off for our first ride together, solo.

Immediately, Chance had his ears forward, alert and relaxed, taking it all in. We rode through a patch of woods and through some puddles following an old road. He really seemed to be enjoying himself. We came out and went down another road, steady and calm. As time went by, I learned that he loves to go on rides in the woods.

The plan was to give him some exercise a little at a time every few days to help get him back in condition after recovering from his sore joint. He walked easily and did not show any sign of favoring his leg. We rode about an hour, and I turned him towards the gate.

Now, some horses are known to run or "bolt" back to the barn as the ride is ending. Not Chance. He seemed like he didn't want the ride to end. He wanted to turn back and keep riding. We were able to work this out and get through gates and back to the barn. I gave him a little alfalfa hay as a reward.

As I pondered the ride, it seemed like the saddle was going downhill. A little low in the front and a little high in the back. The logical fix for this seemed to be to rig the saddle in the three-quarter position. I found later that the better fix was using breast collar. Did I mention how much I had forgotten about things such as this?

Two days later, I decided to take Chance out again. I saddled him in the new seven-eighths position, which moved the saddle a little further forward. It looked a lot better to me. Again, I used the manure bucket as a mounting block. I still had a little difficulty getting into the offhand stirrup and, of course, if I leaned down to guide it, Chance took this a signal to move out. He seemed a little bunched up, which I took as excitement about going on another ride.

Through the gate and leading him down the road, I walked down into the ditch. As he moved down into the ditch, he bounced a little.

"That's odd," I thought. "He's usually so quiet."

Chance was trying to tell me something and I was missing it.

Once inside the lease gate, I tried to use the little mound of dirt, but Chance kept moving away. We were both getting a little agitated. Finally, I was able to get up but missed the offhand stirrup, even as Chance started to bow up and hop a little. In a moment, I left the saddle and was falling toward a hard packed dirt road leading with my, uh… backside. I thought, "This is going to hurt." I landed hard — very hard. It did hurt.

In that moment it went through my head that maybe this horse thing wasn't a great idea for a guy my age. As I got to my feet the other thought was, maybe I should just take him back to the barn. Then the old cowboy thinking rushed in. "NO! Get back on that horse!" I chastised Chance (unfortunately, it wasn't really his fault), led him over to the gate, and checked the girth. After we both calmed down, I was able to lead him to the mound of dirt and we set off for a little ride. I had a nagging feeling that this ride was literally going to be a "pain in the butt!" I wasn't wrong; the pain lingered for a couple of weeks. Some lessons hurt.

As Chance moved out, he still seemed bothered though he settled down and we rode for about an hour. We returned home without further incident. Patty came out to meet us and I told her about the fall. She was concerned; she had already come to love Chance, too, and hoped we could work it out.

If you are an experienced rider or trainer, you have probably already figured out what Chance's problem was and how he tried to tell me several times. You see, with the saddle cinched in the seven-eighths position, it was up on his withers. While the saddle seemed more stable and didn't look like it was running downhill, it was irritating his withers and his shoulders. He first tried to tell me this at the barn, then when the saddle rode up on him going down in the ditch, and finally when I fell off trying to mount at the lease. It is really a testament to his patience that he endured our ride.

When I finally figured this out, I decided to make some changes. First, I fitted the saddle to Chance without a pad and slid my fingers under the front of the saddle to feel for his scapula (shoulder blade). I moved the saddle back until I could feel his shoulder just under the first concho, which is where the edge of the saddle tree is. It was immediately obvious that the saddle had been too far forward, so I re-rigged the saddle to the full position. Second, I raised the stirrups a notch to have a better seat position. Third, I twisted the stirrups around and placed a broom handle through them to help the offhand stirrup turn out to accept the toe of the boot. Fourth, I bought a mounting block for the barn.

The other thing I decided was that a mounting block was needed at the lease. There was a large pine tree that had fallen at the entrance to the lease, so I cut a portion off the stump and hauled it inside the gate with the tractor. I dug a hole and planted it where I could use it as a mounting block inside the lease. It was the perfect solution.

My fall wasn't really Chance's fault; he was reacting to discomfort. I think the most important advancement that we have made in our relationship with horses is to learn that most horses are not really trying to be difficult. The difficulties arise when we fail to read them and understand when something is irritating them or scaring them. They want to trust us; hopefully we can be trustworthy. I wonder if this same approach applies to people who seem difficult? Maybe it's just a misunderstanding?

Though it was a very painful lesson for me, Chance didn't seem the worse for wear and he still trusted me. He was ready to be obedient, and my job would be to know what I was doing so I could read him well and ensure his comfort.

The Third Time's the Charm

I HAVE TO SAY IT wasn't without some consternation that I planned my next ride with Chance. I was still sore from our last encounter. However, pain has a way of underscoring important lessons.

I now had the mounting block in place and some treats on hand. One of Dede's tricks with Chance was to give him a "cookie" after getting up in the saddle. He would stand and turn his head, looking for the cookie. This way he wouldn't move out too soon. It seemed like it was worth a try.

I also enlisted Patty's help. She was to stand and hold his head as I mounted him. Another thought came to me. I know my neighbors pretty well and we have large front yards. I didn't think anyone would mind if Chance and I rode across the edge of the lawn to be a little further away from the road. Then I thought, if Patty could open the gates, I could ride right through and give Chance some time to forget about our re-mount issue at the lease gate. Thankfully, she agreed to all. While I rode, she would be doing some errands so Chance and I would need to ride for about 2 hours if Patty was to open the gates for us on our return.

I put a handful of cookies in my pocket and went out to saddle Chance. As always, he came up to me as soon as I came through the side gate and walked with me to the hitching post. I tied him up and carefully placed the saddle in the proper place, pulling up the pad in front so as not to pinch him. I cinched up the girth and put on the bridle, taking care to see the mane and ears were not being pulled.

Then I said, "Cookie." He could smell them and was eager to take one. I then walked him around a little and back to the hitching post. What do you know, the girth was a little loose, and so I pulled it up a notch. I walked him over to the mounting post and got Patty into position. Chance stood still. I was wearing boots with a real pointed toe and the offhand foot found the stirrup without any problem. I told Patty to release him and said, "Cookie?" He turned his head and took the cookie and with that, we eased off down the pasture. I signaled to Patty that everything was ok and went out through the gate. She opened the lease gate and Chance and I rode through, easy, calm, and relaxed. I checked my watch; it was 1:15 pm.

We rode down the roads and up the roads, sometimes at a little jog. The shorter stirrups felt just right, with my knees in the right position to grip the horse and my lower legs free to signal him. We sloshed through water, examined a menacing old tire, and noticed a few hunting blinds.

Chance was alert, watchful, ears forward, but he didn't spook. I would talk with him about each obstacle and say, "Steady on." Once clear, "Good boy," with a pat on the neck. We were learning to trust each other more and more.

It was getting time to head back to the gate when my cell phone started ringing. Chance paid no attention. I dug it out of my pocket, and it was Patty saying she was at the gate. I told her we were just a few hundred yards away.

"Gary. Gary, turn him around," I heard. Doing so, I saw one of my neighbors with a couple of guys in a side-by-side. Not wanting to spook the horse, they had stopped and called to get my attention. We turned around and rode up to the side-by-side and Chance reached over for a nose rub. Chance stood still as we chatted, then we moved around to the rear of the vehicle. They started up and moved off towards the gate as we followed. Spook Chance? Not likely.

Patty was waiting for us at the gate, and we rode through and down the road to the pasture. We rode right up to the barn, and I dismounted. Chance was calm and stood firm. "Cookie?" Chance looked around and got another cookie.

I mused that this horse thing just might work out after all. What a great ride!

Having begun to read Chance successfully and get the right placement of the saddle, this was the beginning of many great rides. I noticed that I came back relaxed and ready to rest. Chance seemed relaxed as well. We were becoming a good team.

Eventually I mentioned the problem of the old saddle to my sister. She and I began to look around for something that would fit us both a bit better — Chance does have fairly wide withers. After looking around for a while, Dede decided to sell me a saddle that she had used on Chance. It was in good shape and well broken in. It was a Reinsman with a breast collar and back girth, and it does fit him well. It also gives me better feet position and more room. Eventually, I added some saddle bags. I was a little irritated one day when Chance passed too close to the gate post and ripped the stitches, but I will share that part of the story a little later.

Dennis the Menace

DID I MENTION THAT CHANCE is smart? Sometimes too smart for his own good. Dede cautioned me that he likes to scatter stuff around, like tools and other items that he can reach. Gary, my brother-in-law, had added, "If you're doing something, he'll be right in your pocket."

Oh, if we could only listen and learn, our learning would be easier. It has been said that if we don't learn the easy lessons, they get harder.

My first observation of this was when I had the side-by-side parked in front of the barn and Chance came by to investigate. I looked up to see him pulling at some old feed bags in the bed of the side-by-side.

"Hey! What are you doing?" Chance continued unconcerned. I moved towards him and he reluctantly – almost playfully – moved off. It was as if he had found a new game. I pulled the feed bags out and placed them in the hay room.

I went back to my project and Chance went into his stall. He had already finished off the morning's hay.

I suppose in his mind, if I was in the barn, it was time for him to be fed. Periodically, he would give his feed bucket a thump. When this wasn't getting my desired attention, he would thump the stall board with his forefoot. I was a little concerned that he might harm himself, so I chastised him.

I mentioned he likes to eat. Well, he continued doing everything he could think of to get me to throw him some hay or some grain. Of course, from my background, I knew that this behavior should not be rewarded.

Finally, I had enough. I went around and pushed him out of the stall and closed the gate. "There," I thought, "that should settle it."

I went back to the project and heard Chance around by the side-by-side. He was thumping something with his nose. I looked up and saw he had my cell phone in his mouth. I turned towards him, and he dropped it. Again, just a little tweak to let me know he didn't like not being fed on demand. Well, too bad. Sometimes we all have to wait a little while. However, I kept the cell phone with me.

Chance is always watching, always thinking. I think of him sometimes as being like a big dog the way he follows me around, and what sometimes may look like mischief is simply him wanting attention and to engage in play.

I was working on a light over his stall one afternoon. Chance was right there taking it all in. No sooner had I walked away to pick up a tool, he would reach over the stall and knock over the ladder. I would admonish him, and it almost looked like he grinned at me.

Back on the ladder, with my legs at his eye level, he began checking out my pockets. Finding the cell phone, he started nudging it. I don't know what it is with this horse and cell phones. I hope he doesn't expect to be added to my data plan. I would reach down and move him away and he would come right back. He didn't nip or bite, he was just interacting with his "herd mate."

No matter what's going on, he's on top of it. He interacts with the cows over the fence and the neighbor's kids on the other side. In fact, more than once I have come out to feed him and he is looking over the back fence at a gathering of calves. It almost appears as if they are getting a lesson from the teacher.

Chance likes to monitor everything. The vegetable garden is just over the fence in the back corner. I was tilling the garden with the tractor and Chance came over to watch. The tiller can be a clunky and noisy piece of equipment. As I backed down to till another row he was standing there with his head over the fence. As the tiller engaged, he wheeled around, put his head down and gave a little kick. It *looked* like he was afraid, but I think he was just making a statement.

Chance is an outgoing, friendly sort who seems to regard all living things as part of his "herd." Indeed, my sister says that Patty and I *are* his herd. He greets us enthusiastically whenever we approach the pasture gate and even when we come home. Dede calls Chance an "extrovert."

Some of his "Dennis the Menace" behaviors seem to simply be driven by his curiosity and desire to be a part of everything that is going on around him.

Once, while installing the hay rack in his stall, I tried to put him out of his stall. He returned immediately. Some horses would be spooked or put off by someone working in their stall. Chance almost seemed like he was supervising. As I measured and marked and drilled, he was taking in all in. Even when I went over to saw a couple of boards, Chance kept an eye on things. As I was installing the rack and tightening the bolts, he would bend his head around where he could inspect the backside of the rack. He seemed to approve. As soon as the hay was in the rack, he knew just what to do. I gathered my tools and left him to enjoy his new rack.

Chance is a good friend and usually quite docile and accommodating, but he does have a bit of an ornery side at times. It is a bit like a teenager who doesn't take well to being told NO or being corrected. Many times when I fuss at him, he will wheel around, put his head down and kick up his heels in defiance. He doesn't seem to intend any harm, just to convey that he is annoyed!

His independence and desire for his own way often get him into difficulty. Then, like the overly independent teenager, he looks to me to get him out of trouble. Like the day I came out to the barn, and he was standing out front but did not come to greet me. It seems he had been exploring something over the ropes and had his front leg caught. Calmly he waited for me to approach and extract him from his predicament.

On another occasion I had a load of hay on the trailer in the breezeway covered with a tarp. I reasoned that with the rope fence up at either end and the tarp covering the hay that I could return later and put it away. Not with Dennis the Menace. The tarp still has holes where he helped himself. I guess like many horses, he loves to eat.

This also manifested itself in another way. I have a lot of tractor equipment around the barn and do my best to keep it out of Chance's way. The big tiller sits just inside the barn behind some ropes, which Chance usually respects. The tiller has a way of getting dirt into the end of the PTO shaft which makes it really hard to connect to the tractor. One day I thought I had the brilliant idea of placing an old, empty, treat bag over the end of the PTO shaft to keep the dirt out.

The next day, I came out to find that Chance had one foot caught in the rope and the treat bag was shredded. I guess horses have a keener sense of smell than I realized. Chance is never bashful about helping himself. Even so, he stood still for me to get him untangled from the rope and then promptly went around to his stall for his morning grain.

I don't know if this is a universal problem with horses, but they seem to be unaware of the extra space it takes for the rider. Some of my friends have recounted stories of being taken under a branch or scraped on a tree.

My daughter Bonnie is convinced that Chance is a killer and not to be trusted. She was riding him one day at my sister's place and Chance was getting tired of being passed around. They were coming back to the barn and it looked to Bonnie as though he was going to run her into a tree, so she bailed out of the saddle and found herself with a sore arm. Unfortunately, her sore arm was actually broken. Now, years later, my grandson Liam is forbidden from riding the killer horse. Poor Chance… poor Liam.

Poor Chance! Now look what you've done. As we were coming through the pasture gate Chance left just enough room for himself but not enough for the saddle bag. "You've ripped out the stitches on my new saddle bags!" He just looked at me with that blank, "Whatever you say, Boss" look. Fortunately, I have the skills and tools to fix it.

Most folks I talk to say that you have to be on the alert because horses just don't seem to be aware of the rider and the extra gear so they can allow room. It seems as long as they can get through, nothing else matters.

The Bond

FORMER PRESIDENT RONALD REGAN IS quoted as saying, "I've often said there's nothing better for the inside of a man, than the outside of a horse." Please understand that the Former President wasn't excluding women, it was just a form of speech.

Horses have such an amazing way of connecting with us that there is a developing movement of using them as therapy animals. Groups from autistic children to veterans suffering from PTSD have reaped the benefits of this special bond between horse and rider.

Indeed, I remember another horse from my youth; we called him "Buck." It seemed obviously appropriate for a buckskin. We believed him to be a "senior" horse, over 12 years old, when he came to us. He was about 15 hands, alert, steady and basically unflappable.

In those days, my little sister was about 8 years old. She had her own little saddle that we would put on Buck, and he would stand completely still while she pulled every piece of leather available to climb up on him. Once seated, feet in the stirrups, she would kick his sides and say, "Come on, Buck!" The old horse would oblige and move out *carefully*. More than once I heard our parents say that Buck was the best babysitter they ever had.

Buck wasn't incapable of rising to the occasion with an experienced rider. Dad would take him as his mount for hunting. Buck seemed to know we were looking for deer and often when his head turned and the ears went up, Dad would follow his gaze and spot the deer that Buck was watching. Moving through the woods, Buck wouldn't hesitate to leap over a brush pile, which often had Dad grabbing leather.

Dad was a softy when it came to Buck, and it almost led to a serious injury for both one day. As I have said, this bond of trust between the horse and rider is one that relies on each other to make good choices.

One cold, late December morning, it was bright and clear with the temperatures around freezing. Buck didn't want to wade through the cold water to go around a bridge. The water wasn't that deep, but Dad relented to allow Buck to walk across the three-plank section of the bridge. Such bridges often consist of two railroad ties on one side and three on the other. We had often crossed this bridge in this fashion. I was riding behind them and saw Buck's inside back hoof miss the edge of the plank and horse and rider fell into the center of the bridge.

There was a sickening crunch as Buck lunged up to pull himself out. Dad said later he thought it was his leg. Once horse and rider had managed to get free, we could see that the source of the crunch was the stock on Dad's new rifle that had been in the scabbard. It was bent at a 45-degree angle where it had caught the underside of the bridge as Buck tried to come up. Neither the horse nor rider seemed seriously injured. We started a fire so they could warm up and I returned to camp to retrieve another rifle.

When I returned, Dad said that old Buck had been standing close to the fire. We continued on with the hunt. As the day wore on, Dad began to feel more and more pain in his leg. Since I wasn't old enough to drive home, we left early. As it turns out, Dad had suffered a bad bruise.

Both horse and rider learned from the experience. Buck didn't refuse to go through the water again and Dad didn't turn soft and allow the old horse to lead.

You see, horses are herd animals, and they rely on each other and the leader of the herd to keep them safe. In some respects, we as horse owners and riders become the trusted leader.

In the animal world you find those that are predators and those that are prey. Generally, the predators have their eyes positioned in their heads to look forward. Prey animals, those that must avoid the predators, have eyes to the side of their heads to give them maximum peripheral vision to avoid attack. Horses, cows, sheep, and deer have eyes set in this fashion. The horse's instinct when threatened is to run away. The rider can manage this if they have the horse's trust.

I have heard it said that a horse can walk past something like an old tire to the left with no problem, only to return and be spooked by it when it appears on the right side. It seems these two sides are almost independent of each other.

When the horse approaches a puddle, they don't know if it is a few inches deep or several feet deep. They can't tell if it is just a bit of water, or something to turn away from. If the rider has earned the horse's trust, they can get the horse to move through the water or past the obstacle. It is not about *forcing* your will upon the horse; rather it is the horse responding with trust to your judgement and commitment to look after the safety of both.

Early on, Chance and I had to work on this. We would come to a puddle that I knew was only inches deep. I would urge him forward, "Steady on." Tentatively, he would put his head down and move forward. After a few times, he began to trust that I wasn't going to lead him astray. Even so, the rider is smart to note the horse's concern and evaluate a hesitation. The horse may see something that you don't. This is the essence of the bond of trust.

Horses seem to be able to size a person up fairly quickly. If you are calm and confident, they seem to be drawn to you as someone worthy of trust and leadership. If a rider is to guide the horse, the horse must find the rider worthy of that guidance. On the other hand, those that are fearful and timid will cause the horse to be wary and turn away. Once this fear response is started, the horse will not trust the rider but will trust its own survival instincts to fight or flee.

So, the bond of trust between the horse and rider develops over time as the horse trusts the rider and the rider trusts the horse. Activities like feeding, dressing a wound, and grooming, as well as riding, strengthen this bond.

I remember one ride on a pleasant weekday afternoon, Chance and I set off through the dirt roads in the woods. There was such a calm, relaxed feeling between us. His ears were up but he was not hyper alert, just taking it all in. I felt relaxed and at ease in the saddle, guiding him with a nudge from my leg here and there on a loose rain. Chance seemed to really be enjoying himself and I was thoroughly enjoying him.

With confidence we went down some side trails exploring. We would stop from time to time to evaluate our next path. Chance would wait patiently for instruction, sometimes sneaking a mouthful of grass. Once I chose the path, Chance would immediately comply with the direction.

We came upon an armadillo. Chance actually noticed it first. He was watchful as we started around the little creature who then noticed us. "Steady on," I said. Chance relaxed his neck and turned back to the trail. He trusted me that he wouldn't be harmed, and I trusted him to carry me on.

On another occasion we were looking for a short cut out of the woods and back to the house. I thought I saw what looked like an old road or a trail. Then Chance stopped abruptly. I looked down and one front foot was on the other side of a strand of barbed wire. We had ridden into a barbed wire fence concealed by the brush.

I carefully dismounted and talked to Chance is a quiet voice, hiding my concern. He stood motionless as I came around to guide his foot out of the barbed wire. Fortunately, there were no scratches and he seemed none the worse for wear. I swung up in the saddle and took the long way home.

I felt bad for sending him into danger. On the other hand, it was very affirming that he trusted me to find a way out of a bad situation. Trust builds over time. Horses can certainly read us, and our demeaner and tone of voice really matter. Chance understood that we could manage this situation and he didn't need to exert a lot of force. He trusted me to help him figure it out and guide him out of a bad situation.

On yet another ride, we were riding through the roads in the hunting lease. I had not counted on the flies being as bad as they were. I felt bad for Chance and decided that we would go out the south gate and ride back along the highway. As we emerged from the gate onto a dirt road, there was a herd of cattle in the field next to the road. There was also a donkey. If you don't know, donkeys and burros will often graze with cattle, and they are fiercely protective.

As we came up on the road the donkey came toward the fence in a very purposeful way. I was both amused and concerned with Chance's reaction. He was genuinely afraid of the little animal. I reassured him and was able to coax him down the road, past some trees, and Chance carried on.

I guess this nixes the idea we had of getting a donkey as a pasture pal for Chance. Too bad. We thought we would call it "Chancer's Beast."

Horses get the real message, not like humans who can send mixed messages. The horse will sense what is really going on. It seems at times people will say one thing while feeling another. I guess that's why it seems hard to trust some people.

Do You Want... a Cookie?

WHEN CHANCE AND I FIRST rode together at my sister's place, I noticed that she would give him cookies at certain times. First, when she first swung into the saddle, he would turn his head and wait patiently for a cookie before moving out. I later realized this was a great way to ensure that I was ready to ride before he lifted the first hoof.

I mentioned he loves to eat and will begin to salivate when he thinks he is going to get a cookie. I always keep a bag handy. Usually apple flavored, though he also likes molasses... but I imagine he will eat anything. When we go for our rides, he quickens his pace as we visit the neighbor and Chance spies the handyman. Chance knows he is a soft touch for a cookie when we ride up. Sure enough, Chance can usually score at least one cookie, sometimes two!

Over time we developed a routine for our ride in which he would get about 6 cookies. He learned the routine and would be expecting them. If I forgot, he would be a bit miffed but would usually forgive me especially if I made it up at the end of the ride.

We gradually evolved a certain practice of leaving the pasture gate open for our return and I tried to teach Chance that I wanted him to work with me on closing the gate. It was frustration for both of us. Then one day he seemed to get the picture as if to say, "Boss, I got this!" As we moved around to the backside of the gate Chance nosed it shut, turned to his left, and brought me up to the post on the right side so I could drop the latch over the post. From then on, this is how we return from our ride. I was so impressed that when I dismounted to secure the gate, I gave him a cookie.

So, when we are getting ready for a ride as I appear with his halter and lead and say, "Do you want... a cookie?" Chance begins to salivate and come to me. He puts his head into the halter, I secure it, and he gets his cookie.

Then I lead him over to the big oak tree and tie him off. He gets brushed and saddled. When I am ready to bridle him, he willingly puts his head in the bridle, licking his lips. "Do you want... a cookie?" And he gets... a cookie. That's two.

Moving over to the mounting block, he stands quietly, and I step into the saddle. "Do you want... a cookie?" He bends his head around and gets... a cookie! Number three. We set off for the front gate. I dismount and prop it open and lead him into a shallow ditch to make it easier to mount, and we are off on our ride.

As I mentioned, when we ride by the neighbor's place Chance looks for Richard, the handyman, and if he spies him, he quickens his pace, knowing that it is likely he will get a bonus cookie. Richard will say, "Chance, do you want a cookie?" He licks his lips and Richard gives him a cookie. My sister would usually reward him at the mid-point in their ride with another cookie, but I like to keep him guessing.

When we arrive back at the front gate, he stops for me to release the prop and we turn inside, and I allow him to close the gate for me. Once the gate is closed, I dismount and say, "Do you want... a cookie?" He gets another cookie!

Back at the barn, I remove the bridle and hang it on the saddle and wait for him to stop rubbing his head on the oak tree. Chance then puts his head into the halter, and I proceed to unsaddle him. He waits patiently as I put away the tack and brush him down.

I usually give him a small ration of grain and a bit of fresh hay as a reward for the ride. As I come around, I will say, "I have two cookies for good horses. Do you know any good horses?"

Immediately he begins to salivate and lick his lips. He gets his first cookie as I untie the lead from the tree. Then, to keep him from bolting to his stall, I put the lead around his neck and remove the halter. He waits, less patiently, and he gets the last cookie. I release the rope and he turns toward the barn.

So, on a typical ride he will get 6 or 7 cookies, sometimes more if Richard is in a generous mood and Chance endears himself.

I suppose, if I were an imaginative and skilled horse trainer, with Chance's love for cookies I could probably teach him all kinds of tricks. He loves his rides, especially in the woods, and he seems happy enough, but… he *loves* his cookies!

When Chance Met Chick-Chick

ONE SUMMER DAY WE WENT out to the barn and my wife Patty noticed a little bantam hen scratching around the barn. We were puzzled because the only people we knew who had chickens were our neighbors to the north. We contacted them and asked them if they were missing any chickens; they said "no."

Patty, a bonified animal lover, thought the chicken looked thirsty so she brought out a pan of water and the chicken began to drink. We offered it the only thing we had that a chicken might be interested in, some oats. This was a mystery. Where did the chicken come from and who did it belong to? I mentioned it to our immediate neighbor to the north and they said that their son had captured the chicken at their dad's workplace, noting that there were lots of them running around. They intended to keep it as a pet, but the chicken didn't seem to want to hang out around their place during the day, preferring to scratch around after the horse and look for bugs.

This turned out the be a mutually satisfactory arrangement as the chicken was making a mess of their patio. It would roost on the satellite dish over their bedroom window and often make a ruckus at night, which did not please them either.

Patty named the chicken Chick-Chick and bought an expensive galvanized water dispenser so that Chick-Chick would always have access to fresh water.

Patty wanted Chick-Chick to have a proper coop and perch. I asked the neighbor if they were okay with that and they indicated, due to the mess and the noise, they were more than okay with it.

After some research, I set out to build a coop complete with a ramp. The ramp had little oak cleats every few inches to ensure that Chick-Chick could easily walk up into the coop. The cost of materials was about $150. (The ramp alone was $20.)

All the while Chance seemed to welcome the company. He was careful not to move too quickly around Chick-Chick and seemed rather curious about his new pasture pal.

Well, little did I know this was only the beginning. Soon to follow was an egg box and Chick-Chick began producing eggs. Patty had always wanted chickens, so she soon found someone and acquired three more chickens. Now this constituted the need for a large coop.

As time went by, we acquired a flock of chickens. They follow Chance around the pasture waiting to scratch through the manure. Chance seems mindful of them and careful not to step on them.

Now that we had more chickens, we had to have a bigger coop. I moved all the tractor implements out of the southwest corner of the barn and proceeded to enclose it with wire, eventually making a 10-foot by 12-foot coop with elaborate roosts and more egg boxes.

As usual, Chance monitored everything with keen interest. He took every opportunity to sample the chicken feed and, on several occasions, would sneak into the coop when Patty left the big door open to go in and clean the coop and tend to the feed and water. Dennis the Menace, at it again.

All the while, Chance seemed careful and interested in Chick-Chick and his new pasture pals – even when they invaded his stall to kick the mature around. (A practice I try to minimize by getting the manure picked up before the chickens are let out of the coop.)

The chickens keep coming and Chance doesn't seem to mind. Mostly they use the egg boxes, but they will also lay eggs where the hay is stored and even jump up into Chance's hayrack to lay eggs there. We keep trying to discourage them from these alternative places, but Chance doesn't seem to mind. Chick-Chick and the others are just part of the herd.

We do have one unusual chicken that we have acquired along the way. She is a Rhode Island Red and, I suppose like many people, we call her Rosey. She has become the lead chicken, usually the top of the pecking order. She is usually first on the scene around Chance, who doesn't seem to mind. She does have one special trick. When we go out to the barn and say, "Rosey the Chicken!" she will flap her wings as if in a greeting.

Speaking of herds, another neighbor keeps cattle in the field behind Chance's stall. In the spring, when the calves are being born, it is not uncommon to arrive at the barn for the morning feeding and find Chance looking out upon a group of young calves gathered at the fence as if he is teaching school. I think it is comforting for Chance to have so many other creatures around. We have often thought of getting another horse, or even a donkey. We thought of calling the donkey, "Chancer's Beast," but so far, we just have Chance.

As I have said, Chance is an extrovert. He loves to interact with people and all kinds of other creatures. That is except one. He doesn't like hogs.

Chance Doesn't Like Hogs

ONE EARLY FALL DAY, CHANCE and I were riding around the neighbor's property when Chance spun around to his left and we almost became separated. I was a bit puzzled because Chance is usually very steady. Standing there, he was trembling and ready to bolt. He kept flaring his nostrils and breathing as if trying to smell something.

As I looked around, I saw that the neighbor had a pen where a girl was raising a hog for the county fair. I was to learn later that the hog was really quite friendly. Chance would have none of it. We detoured out and around where the pen was to continue our ride.

On a couple of occasions, I was able to bribe Chance with extra cookies, but he still wasn't comfortable with the situation. The hog seemed totally disinterested in the whole thing.

I began doing a little research and listening to other horse owners. It turns out that lot of horses are not fond of pigs and would rather avoid them. Speculation about this includes the fact that feral hogs can be rather aggressive and have been known to attack horses and drive them away from food sources. Not to mention the fact that, most of the time, hogs have a particular smell about them. Horses are surprisingly on the alert for smells they associate with danger.

As I said, Chance is usually very steady. He doesn't seem to mind walking by the beehives that are set out in the woods during the spring. We are always careful, keep our distance, and go by slowly, but he doesn't have nearly the reaction to the bees as he does to hogs.

All things being equal, I am basically pleased with Chance and his usual good nature, I decided to accept this quirk as it seems to be somewhat common to horses.

Later that fall, I was hunting out of a "condo stand." That's an enclosed, raised stand set up over a food plot. I usually try to take a deer and a hog each year for the freezer. I had not had an opportunity to take a hog yet that season.

In the distance on the neighbor's property, I saw a small herd of nice hogs crossing into the woods to the left of my stand. I was hoping they would come on to the food plot, but they were just beyond it. I wondered where they were crossing and if I could find a way to intercept them in the future.

Then I remembered Chance's reaction to the smell of hogs. During the middle part of the day, especially during the week, we don't have many hunters on the property. I thought, if Chance and I could come down the back road and check out the trails, I might find where the hogs are coming through.

I went home and saddled Chance and we worked our way down the roads to this back road.

We started going down the trails. The first one looked promising but no reaction, then another … nothing. Finally, we started down a trail and Chance flared his nostrils and became rather nervous. I was able to reassure him, and we set out for home. I thought to myself, well besides being a good friend and a nice ride, Chance is a pretty reliable hog dog! Truly it seems horses have a good sense of smell.

Please Take Me to the New Pasture?

MY WIFE PATTY IS A bit like the old Texas Rancher who only wanted to buy what joined him. She first bought the 1.5-acre lot to the north of us, the one where we put up the barn. Then she began talking with the lady on our south side and learned that she planned to move back to Ohio when she retired.

As the time drew near for the lady to retire, Patty made it known that she was interested in the property. It seemed that they might be able to work out a deal. When the time came for the lady to begin packing, someone stopped by and began to negotiate for the property. That evening, the lady came by and knocked on the door to tell Patty what she wanted for the property, and she would sell it to whoever came up with the money first. I told Patty she'd better get a contract drawn up and she called a realtor friend that night and had the contract ready the next day.

The other fella was not too happy about it. But we did get the property and remained on good terms with our neighbor.

I was in need of some office space, and we thought that the mobile home would be a good solution. That is, until we learned that we could not insure it if no one lived there and that the county would tax it separately from the land which we added to our homestead. When the air conditioner went out, that was the last straw, and we began looking for someone to buy the mobile home and move it off of the property.

Meanwhile, I had found a beautiful oak desk at a consignment shop. It took four of us to load in the back of the pickup. When I got it home, it was just me and Patty... well mostly just me. Having what I call a PhD in Redneck Engineering, I decided to put the forks on the tractor to lift the desk out of the truck and up onto the deck of the mobile home. I carefully slid the forks under the desk and ran straps around it to hold against the upright part of the forks. It actually went pretty well except that I couldn't get close enough to the deck because of the stair rails. With the help of a come-a-long and some dollies, I was able to move it onto the deck and into the mobile home where Patty helped me set it up on its legs.

Imagine my consternation when it was decided that we needed to sell the mobile. I began the extraction process and moved the desk into an old shed on the property where it sat for several months.

Once the new building was ready, I carefully slid the forks under the desk, strapped it down, and brought it over. I carefully maneuvered the desk through the door and with the help of a couple of dollies and Patty, we were able to move it into position. A position from which I am typing just now.

The move into the new building was delayed a bit. You see, as we began to process of putting up a building that would cover the truck and have an enclosed space, we ran into some difficulty with the building department that took about six months to resolve. Six months later, the building was up, and I was ready to fence the new pasture. Many of the materials I needed had almost doubled in price since my last fence project.

I managed to find a couple of old telephone poles to use for anchors and gate posts. In addition to fencing the pasture I had to put up something around the well to keep Chance from exploring, as well as a cover over the controls for the septic tank. Finally, it was done, and I put down lime and fertilizer just as the spring rains set in. It came up lush and green.

The first time I walked Chance across the yard to the new pasture, he was excited and licking his lips. I don't think he lifted his head all day. He didn't seem to know where to graze first. He was one happy horse. Reluctantly, he would meet me at the gate to go over to the barn to get his evening grain and hay.

I remember several days hearing the sound of pounding hooves to look out and find Chance running around the new pasture. He reveled in his new space.

Chance began to get the routine down pretty quick – he is smart. After completing the morning chores at the barn, I was walking to the gate and I heard the thunder of hooves. I was a little concerned to hear Chance approaching at a run. Not only was he running, but Chance was whickering for all he was worth as if to say, "Take me to the new pasture!"

This became a thing where Chance would finish his grain and ignore his hay to be sure I would walk him over to the new field. Sometimes he is quite ready in the morning and the first time he sees me outside he will come to the gate and whicker. Off course, I oblige and walk him over. The things we do for our horses!

One morning I went out to walk Chance over to the pasture. He was loafing in his stall. I went through the gate and decided I didn't need to close it completely as Chance would be waiting for me. Usually, he will wait for me to get to his stall to see what I am up to. On this particular morning, I walked into the breezeway and picked up his halter. As I have said, most times he will wait and put his head right into the halter. Not today.

As I moved through the breezeway he came out of his stall and started to walk away. I was immediately concerned because I knew the gate was ajar. I approached and Chance moved away. I got him into a corner, and he suddenly bolted past me right for the gate.

I hoped that he would just run across the yard to the other pasture gate. Nope! He headed straight for the road.

We live on a pretty busy road. Log trucks and all kinds of traffic speed by. Fortunately, today the traffic was fairly light. I heard a big truck coming around the corner and to my relief the driver saw the situation and stopped. Chance was grazing at the side of the road. As I approached him, BOZO took off, right down the side of the road.

I was just imagining all the things that could happen. I called Patty on my phone and simply said, "I need help. Chance got out."

The he turned into the neighbor's driveway. It was fenced on both sides with a gate. Chance went to the front lawn and started grazing, I came through the gate and closed it. "Now I've got you," I thought.

Chance now had begun to think that this was some kind of game. He moved around the side of the house. I circled back to cut him off. Then we were face to face on the neighbor's driveway. "Whoa, whoa," I said. By now Chance realized he was in unfamiliar territory, and he seemed a little nervous and contrite.

I moved in and got the halter on him. He was still a bit nervous, so I tried to speak softly and stay calm as I had to lead him back down the side of the road to the pasture. I could feel him kind of bunched up and knew that if I didn't stay calm, he would probably bolt.

You think you know a horse and then they come up with something like this! I guess you can never be absolutely sure how a horse is going to react, and you should always close the gate.

Come to think of it, he did a similar trick coming back from a ride. He loves to ride through the woods, and I have access to a hunting lease across the road. During the off season we will often take long rides as there are some natural loops we can use.

On this particular ride, I had to stop and open a gate so we could make our way home. Usually, almost 100% percent of the time, if there is any good grass around, Chance will drop his head and try to eat as much of it as he can.

He pulled at the reins to move toward a stand of rich green grass. Being an old softy, I gave him his head. As I turned around from locking the gate, Chance was crossing the highway dragging the reins to the side. I hollered "Whoa" but he ignored me. It was as if he were saying, "Hey Boss! I know where I am, I'll see you back at the barn"... About a mile away.

I fell in behind him and noticed that he was very distracted when he stepped on the reins. I began to make up ground on him. Then, he stepped on both reins, and I quickly reached around and grabbed them.

After chastising him severely, I re-mounted and we made our way home.

Horses, no matter how much you love them, they can always come up with a way to surprise you.

Then, it is hard to hold a grudge when you friend trots over to meet you so that you can take him to the barn for his evening feed. Or when he's just in a real friendly mood and he hangs his head over your shoulder. The times when I am surprised by his actions, I could really count on one hand. He consistently shows his love and appreciation to Patty and me for tending to him, feeding him, loving on him... countless.

Storms, Guns and Bottle Rockets

IF YOU HAVE EVER LIVED in Florida or anywhere in the Southeastern part of the country, you are likely to have experienced some kind of tropical event or a hurricane. Living in North Florida we have had a few come through our area. Usually, it is a lot of wind and rain with occasional power outages.

Most of our outbuildings and barns have metal roofs, which can make a lot of noise in the wind. For a time, our barn had a peculiar way of having the western edge flap in a southwest wind. So much so, in fact, that it began to fatigue the metal. Chance found this particularly annoying and would run out of his stall, even abandoning his feed. I finally figured out a way to reinforce the edge and quiet this problem. Even so, these roofs are noisy with branches scraping against them and acorns falling.

So, when a storm is on the way, the dilemma is whether the horse is better off in the field or in the stall. Most say that, due to the horses' flight tendency, letting them run is probably best. We are just a bit south of Cumberland Island where some wild horses have roamed for many years. They seem to thrive.

When a storm approaches, I make sure that there are no obstacles in the pasture and give Chance plenty of hay and water. The rest is left up to him. So far, he seems to handle it very well... unless something falls on the roof. Then he will exit the stall and kick up his heels in protest.

I have also noticed that as the winds pick up, he will often run around the pasture. My belief is that animals sense the arrival of a low-pressure area, like that associated with a tropical storm or hurricane. I am thinking that with the approach of bad weather, Chance knows that something is up. I worry that if he was not restrained in the pasture, he might give in to his flight tendency and try to run away from the bad weather.

Guns are another matter and rather random. I enjoy watching the re-runs of the Lone Ranger. I notice how he shoots his revolver over the head of his horse, Silver. The horse carries on, and I notice he lays his ears down to minimize the sound of the gun.

I have seen horses that seem to be acclimated to gun shots. There are even competitions in which people shoot at balloons with blanks while riding the horse. I know people who have hunted on horseback, myself included. But I never have taken a shot from the back of a horse.

Chances' responses are varied. Several of my neighbors across the road from us have target ranges in their back yards. As hunting season rolls around, they are out there checking the sights on high powered rifles. This doesn't seem to bother Chance, nor does rapid fire pistol shots. If someone sets of some Tannerite, which makes a rather loud boom, he will look up, continue chewing, and go back to grazing.

Now to the west of us is a large open cow pasture. In the fall, those folks like to hunker down in the tree line on the extreme west side of the field and shoot doves as they come in to roost. This seems to be a problem for Chance. He doesn't start running around, but he will avoid going into his stall during this activity. I wonder if the sound resonates off the metal roof, though it is several hundred yards away.

I am sure that I could take a shot from Chances' back… once. Remembering my earlier, painful lesson, I think I will avoid this activity if at all possible. I always carry some kind of pistol when I go into the woods, but it would have to be an extraordinary circumstance to get me to take a shot while on horseback. Besides, I'd rather not walk home.

Fireworks! Now there's a topic of discussion among horse owners and pet owners alike. In our area of the country, people like to set off fireworks on July Fourth and New Year's Eve. I have read many stories of how horses are spooked by such things, some even to the point of running through a fence or otherwise injuring themselves, sometimes fatally.

I make it a point to be around at these times. When I hear the first boom, I walk out to the pasture to see how Chance is doing. Generally, he will quiet down as I stand with him. Sometimes I have tried to work with my neighbors, and they seem unfazed by Chances' reactions.

I remember one year; I was standing with Chance, and we were watching people across the road set off mortars. They were big and noisy and Chance seemed to be handling it okay. Then one of the launch tubes fell over and the mortal skipped across the road and almost impacted the neighbor's home. Fortunately, there was no damage. This seemed to be a "sobering" reality for the neighbor, and they suspended further launches.

The things that really seem to bother Chance are the bottle rockets. I don't know if it is the peculiar sound they make, or the sound associated with the visual, but he doesn't like them at all. He will stand alert, trembling and, if not reassured, will take off running around the pasture. This is where you hope he is sure footed enough not to stumble or fall into a hole.

It would sure be nice if folks engaged in these activities could appreciate the impact it has on livestock and offer some consideration. I even suggested to the County Commissioners that we come up with something that would give some guidance about setting off fireworks in proximity to livestock, but they didn't think they could get it through.

So, for now, I spend July Fourth and New Year's Eve with Chance, out in the pasture, watching the show.

What if People Were
More Like Horses?

NO, IT'S NOT WHAT YOU'RE thinking, though I suppose there are some people that qualify.

My experience with horses leads me to celebrate their noble nature, their desire to do the right thing. The horses that I have known have been more patient with me than I have been with them at times.

When a horse comes to greet me, it is all about the connection. They seem glad to see me and anxious to know what we will do next. It is never about them, well... unless it is feeding time. So often when people approach us, they seem to have their own agenda of what we can do for them. Even at feeding time, the horse seems grateful that we will be there to take care of them.

Then there is the loyalty factor. With few exceptions, the horses I have known are trusting and loyal to me. They depend on me as I often depend on them, a mutual assistance arrangement. I have known a few people who do seem to want such a partnership. Then too, there are those times when we make mistakes with horses such as I did with Chance. I have found, if you are kind, the horse will forgive and even forget.

People seem to hold on to hurts and affronts, even if they are only their perceptions that wrongs have occurred. They will hold on to them, hoping that it will somehow convince the other person of how they are wrong, in essence trying to punish them.

A friend of mine once said, "Holding on to a grudge hoping someone will give in, is a bit like drinking poison hoping someone else will get sick." That is to say that holding on to bitterness only makes us feel bad. Somehow horses know this, and they seem quick to forgive and ready to move on.

Horses are genuine. They simply are what they are, "what you see is what you get." No attempt to mask their true identity, they are open and present with those they trust. I have to wonder… if people could be that way, would we be having more genuine discussions? Would we be able to listen more and manipulate less? Would we be able to share our thoughts and feelings in ways that lead to solutions rather than conflict?

Yes, what if people could be more like horses? Loving, trusting, genuine able to forgive and eager to connect in a real way…

Is this why horses are so valuable as therapy animals? They know how to be present for those who struggle with things like autism, trauma, and PTSD. They are there, standing silently by ready to be a friend and not needing to know all about the hurt. They are just willing to be present and help one to move forward and to know the joy and the bond of true friendship.

When people talk about these kinds of relationships with horses, you know it is a life changing encounter. This is why it is so hard for the horse and rider to part company, especially for the last time.

We're Still Riding

SOME TIME HAS PASSED SINCE I started writing this book. Chance and I are both a bit older and we still enjoy getting out two or three times a week for a ride. I take it easy on the old guy and he does the same for me. Just a nice walk through the woods. He still can't wait to put his head down into the bridle and get his cookie!

There are times when you know that one day the bond will be broken, one way or another. Still, for me the time spent together is well worthwhile. I suppose there are people who wonder why you would keep animals that you have to feed and care for, that tie you down from taking trips and doing other things. These are the folks who don't understand the simple joy of being greeted at the pasture gate, nuzzled after a good ride, or just being followed around by a good friend.

Even the chickens run to greet us in the afternoon.

Sure, some of this is driven by their desire for their evening feed, but it is always nice to be appreciated.

I think that our animals keep us healthy and honest. We have a reason to get up in the morning knowing that they need to be fed and looked after. Sometimes it feels like a chore but on the whole, I wouldn't trade it for anything else.

Animals can read us and they respond positively to genuineness and kindness. As a minister and mental health counselor, I am often puzzled by the lack of genuineness in some people. It is so easy to deal with animals. It would be so much nicer if people could just be as true and faithful with each other.

Just now, when I went over to the house for something, Chance came to the north gate and whickered as if asking to come over to the south pasture. Of course I obliged… he's worth it.

I actually feel sad for people who have never experienced this kind of connection to an animal. Thankfully, I can't imagine what that empty place is like.

I took a Chance, and I am very happy that I did!

Printed in the United States
by Baker & Taylor Publisher Services